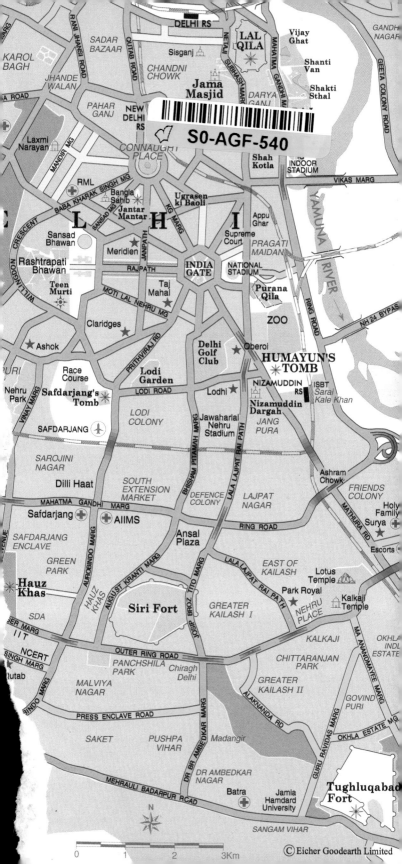

World Heritage Series

HUMAYUN'S TOMB

& ADJACENT MONUMENTS

Based on the text of
S A A Naqvi

प्रलकीर्तिमपावृणु

Published by

The Director General
ARCHAEOLOGICAL SURVEY OF INDIA
New Delhi, 2002

Editor-in-Chief: Swati Mitra
Senior Editor: Sona Thakur
Designer: Sagarmoy Paul

Photographers:
Sagarmoy Paul: pp.15, 28Above, 38-39, 46,
61, 67, 72-75, 77, 78

Shalinee Ghosh: pp.4-13, 34-37, 41A, 44-45, 49-53,
58-60, 62-66, 68-71, 76, 79A, 82

Surendra Sahai: pp.24, 28Below, 31, 32, 55
Cover Photograph: Shalinee Ghosh

Illustrations: Himanish Das pp. 21, 27, 42-43, 80-81
Design Assistance: V Murali

Special thanks to
Umesh Kumar, B R Mani, Arundhati Banerji, Hoshiar Singh
and Purnima Ray of the Archaeological Survey of India, New Delhi,
without whose assistance this book would not have been possible.
Thanks also to Ratish Nanda for his note on Revitalisation of
Humayun's Tomb Gardens.

Conceptualised and Designed by
Good Earth Publications
Eicher Goodearth Limited, New Delhi.
Printed at International Print-O-Pac Ltd, New Delhi

Price: Rs 99

Contents

Preface

to S A A Naqvi, *Humayun's Tomb and Adjacent Buildings*

*T*he mausoleum of Humayun is the first mature example of Moghul architecture. If it were compared with the tomb of the Afghan interloper, Sher Shah Suri, who died shortly before Humayun and was buried at Sasaram in Bihar, the contrast is instructive. Sher Shah's tomb (1539-45) marks the culmination of a fifteenth-century style which had been elaborated by the Lodi dynasty and is represented for the last time at Delhi in the tomb of Isa Khan (1547), close alongside the tomb of Humayun. In its most evolved form, the Lodi tomb was an octagonal structure with one or more tiers of pavilions or *chhatries* piling up to a flat central dome – a trick of design invented in essence long previously at Khajuraho (AD 1000) and elsewhere by the Hindu temple-builders, who had similarly built up the pavilion-roofs of halls and vestibules to support the tall superstructure of the ultimate shrine. The outline of the Lodi tomb was thus strong, and coherent, and its strength was not infrequently emphasised by a ruggedness of masonry that was thinly disguised by plasterwork or tiles.

Humayun's Tomb, on the other hand, discards both the elementary symmetry of the Lodi type and its crude stone cutting. The elevations are dominated by two features derived from Persian architecture: the range of three great arches on each side, and the high, emphatic dome. The high dome is achieved by the use of a double shell – a feature which had been used in Persia perhaps as early as the thirteenth-century (Kirman), but now appears for the first time in India. It is still 'supported' by Hindu pavilions, which were indeed to be incorporated wholeheartedly in the Moghul style; but their grouping is less mechanical than in the Lodi-Sher Shah series, and they do not crowd upon and smother the central feature.

In the perfection of the mason's craft the tomb of Humayun likewise established the Moghul standard. Given good freestone, the Indian mason had always shown an unsurpassed skill in the cutting of masonry. The resources of the Moghul patrons ensured henceforth a constant supply of the best stones and marbles in the empire. In Persia the variegation of the surface of a building was almost invariably left to coloured tiles; in India richly coloured stones and traditional craftsmanship were summoned to supply the need. In this as in other respects the Persian master-builders of the Moghuls adopted and adapted, and the tomb of Humayun illustrates the process in its early perfection.

R E M WHEELER
Director General of Archaeology in India
New Delhi, 1946

Introduction

*H*igh in the snow-sheathed mountains of the Safed Koh is a narrow pass that has seen army after invading army sweep through on its way south into the rich Indo-Gangetic plains. It was through the winding Khyber Pass that Alexander's army marched on its way to conquer the world; it was through here that the Persians, Scythians and Parthians came.

And it was through here that a horde of marauding Mongols came sweeping down in 1398, plundering and laying waste all before them. Their warrior chieftain, Timur, was in India for less than six months but in that time plundered so much that, according to one contemporary account, his army was 'so laden with booty that they could scarce march four miles a day'.

Among the booty Timur took back to Samarkand were a herd of elephants and a team of stone-masons. These soon became part of a community of artists and artisans in Samarkand which already included painters, calligraphers and architects from Persia and would soon be joined by silk weavers and glass blowers from Damascus and silversmiths from Turkey, as soon as Timur overran those lands.

Right:
Arcaded verandah around the main chamber of Isa Khan's Tomb

Cultured court life was an integral part of the Timurid ideal. Books and manuscripts were treasures the Timurid princes seldom let out of their sights; and they delighted in landscaping elegant pleasure gardens. Architecture, too, was a passion and the great cities of Samarkand and Herat were studded with magnificent buildings.

This intertwining of the aesthete and the warrior in the person of the king was an ideal that all Timur's descendants would aspire to, including those history knows as the Mughals. Historian Ebba Koch sums up the humanistic Timurid legacy of the Mughals, saying that they combined 'political and military genius with scientific, artistic, even mystical qualifications of the highest order'. She goes on to categorise them as 'not only founders of cities (Akbar, Jahangir and Shahjahan), architects (Shahjahan), recognised naturalists and horticulturists (Jahangir), polo-players (Akbar, Jahangir) and excellent shots (including Jahangir's wife Nur Jahan), but also authors of readable autobiographies (Babur and Jahangir), letters (Aurangzeb) and poems (Babur); they were calligraphers, collectors of art, sponsors of painting and literature, astronomers (Humayun), religious innovators and authors of philosophical treatises and of mystic works (Dara Shikoh and Jahanara)'.

Right:
Intricate *jali* work on windows inside Humayun's Tomb

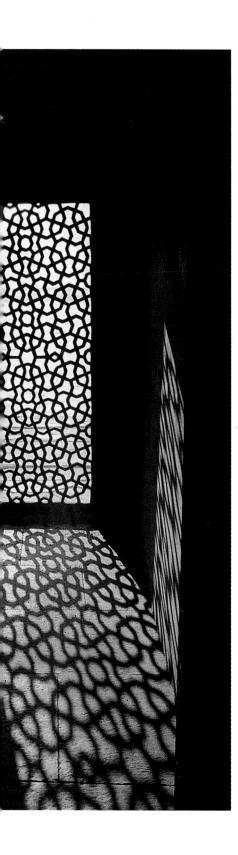

Mughals

1526
Babur
1530
Humayun
1539
Humayun deposed
by Sher Shah

Surs

1539
Sher Shah
1545
Islam Shah
1552
Muhammad Adil
1553
Ibrahim Sur
1554
Sikandar

Mughals

1555
Humayun reinstated
1556
Akbar
1605
Jahangir
1628
Shahjahan
1659
Aurangzeb Alamgir
1707
Bahadur Shah I
1712
Jahandar Shah
1713
Farukkhsiyar
1719
Muhammad
1748
Invasion of
Ahmad Shah Daurani
1748
Ahmad Shah
1754
Alamgir II
1759
Shah Alam
1806
Akbar II
1837
Bahadur Shah II
Uprising of 1857

Babur, the first of the line in India, was quite close to the Timurid ideal. A born warrior, his attack on north India, which he claimed as part of his Timurid legacy, was masterly. Taking advantage of the internecine squabbles among the Afghan rulers of north India, he swept through the mountain passes and was well into Punjab before his enemy could react.

Ibrahim Lodi, the Sultan of Delhi marched out to meet him and the two armies faced each other at Panipat. The Lodi ruler had 100,000 men and a thousand elephants as against Babur's 20,000 soldiers. But Babur had artillery – his musketeers under the command of the Turk, Ustad Ali Quli rained chaos into the ranks of the enemy and Babur won Hindustan in April 1526.

Babur was a true Timurid, with equal measures of martial and artistic skills. He had an abiding passion for books and gardens, and was an accomplished poet. Few of his gardens in India survive, but the *Baburnama* does. This memoir spans Babur's transition from a nomad prince to the emperor of Hindustan.

His son, Humayun, although not lacking in personal courage, was certainly not as able a commander as his father. Historians contend that he never took time out to consolidate a battle victory and would fritter away months celebrating the triumph in an unending feast of wine, opium and poetry.

Right:
Humayun's Tomb

Humayun was uncommonly superstitious (he never entered a room left foot first) and completely star-struck. According to Abul Fazl, he organised the administration of his kingdom on astrological lines, dividing departments according to the elements – Earth looked after agriculture and architecture; Water looked after irrigation and the royal cellars; Fire was in charge of all matters military; and Air was left with miscellaneous subjects like 'the wardrobe, the kitchens, the stables and the necessary management of the mules and camels'.

Each day of the week was reserved for a particular administrative function based on the planet governing the day. So, Tuesday, governed by Mars, was given over to justice, Sunday to affairs of state and Monday to matters of mirth. Humayun, ever-inventive, also had a huge 'carpet of mirth' with astrological symbols and planetary positions marked on it. Courtiers and officers were supposed to arrange themselves on it while Humayun, seated on the Sun, cast dice to get them to disport themselves for his amusement.

To be fair to him, Humayun set about to develop a new city in keeping with the Timurid traditions of his forefathers. Soon after his accession he laid the foundations of a new city by the Yamuna and grandly called it Dinpanah or Refuge of the Faithful.

Right:
The main tomb chamber of Humayun's Tomb

But, that project never saw fruition for he soon lost his kingdom to Sher Shah Sur.

When he managed to regain his patrimony after 15 years in exile, Humayun found that the usurper Sher Shah had completed his city project. He moved into the Sur citadel, today known as Purana Qila, and in fact died there. His temporary tomb or *supurdgah* was also inside the same fort and it was only much later that his remains were moved into the mausoleum his widow, Haji Begum, built for him.

Humayun's Tomb, the first mausoleum for a Mughal emperor, drew inspiration from 15th century Timurid architecture. Built to a meticulously symmetrical plan, it displayed a range of Timurid characteristics, including the bulbous double dome on a high drum; a high portal in the front elevation; coloured tilework arranged geometrically; and arch-netting in the vaults.

Here it combines with decidedly pre-Mughal elements like the combined use of red sandstone and white marble inlay; lotus bud-fringed arches, perforated stone *jali* screens, wide *chhajja* eaves and corbelled ornamental brackets. So, in a sense, the monument of the Humayun's Tomb became an architectural metaphor for the Indianisation of the Mughals.

Right:
The emperor's cenotaph

Purana Qila

*E*mperor Humayun, son of the first Mughal, Babur, ascended the throne of Delhi in 1530. Three years thereafter he laid the foundations of a city he named Dinpanah, or the Refuge of the Faithful. The inner citadel of this city is today known as Purana Qila (Old Fort). Within six years, Humayun was ousted by Sher Shah Sur (1538-45) who promptly renamed the city Shergarh. Sher Shah destroyed Dinpanah and raised a citadel on the same site.

The first six years of Humayun's reign were wrought with continuous strife with provincial governors, not to mention the constant pressure of the Sur sultan. Quite naturally in these circumstances he had no time for artistic or architectural pursuits. So though he laid the foundations of his citadel, it is not known how much building activity had taken place at the site during those years, or how much Sher Shah actually destroyed when he took it over. What is known is that there are no extant buildings from Humayun's first stint as emperor.

Above:
Purana Qila

The location of Purana Qila is not new to history, as the earliest reference to this site is made in the Hindu epic, *Mahabharata*, which states that the Pandavas founded a city called Indraprastha beside the river Yamuna. Recent excavations at Salimgarh in Red Fort and at Purana Qila have yielded Painted Grey Ware pottery which have also been found in other sites associated with the *Mahabharata* and has been dated to around 1,000 BC. The fact that till 1913 there was a village within the fort walls called Indrapat adds credence to the theory that Purana Qila is built on the remains of Indraprastha.

Purana Qila is irregularly oblong on plan, with bastions on the corners and in the western wall. It has three gates – Humayun Darwaza, Talaqi Darwaza ('forbidden gate') and the Bara Darwaza, through which one enters the fort today. The south gate is known as the Humayun Darwaza, not because Humayun built it but probably because Humayun's Tomb is visible through it. Archaeologist Y D Sharma mentions that among the scribblings in ink that existed in a recess at the Talaqi Darwaza there was a mention of Humayun, and it is possible that the gate may either have been constructed by him or at least repaired by him.

Inside Purana Qila is Qala-i-Kuhna Masjid built by Sultan Sher Shah, and certainly one of his finest architectural statements. It is one of the few buildings still extant within Old Fort. The builders must have attempted to complete the central portion in white marble but the scarcity of this material seems to have led them to use deep red sandstone that gives the building a pleasing character.

The inner west wall of the Masjid has five arched openings that are richly ornamented in white and black marble. On a marble slab within the mosque is an inscription which translates as, 'As long as there are people on this earth, may this edifice be frequented and people be cheerful and happy in it.'

Sher Shah also built the Sher Mandal, a two-storeyed octagonal pavilion in red sandstone relieved by marble, probably as a pleasure resort.

Below:
Gateway of the Qala-i-Kuhna Masjid built by Sher Shah Sur

The building has acquired historical importance beyond its architectural merits as Humayun tripped on its tortuous staircase and fell to his death in 1556. It is believed that Humayun used it as his library.

The story goes that the emperor was climbing down when he heard the call of the *muazzin* and seated himself down immediately on the steps. When he got up, his foot caught in his robe and he fell down the steps. His injuries brought about his death soon after.

On the west of Sher Mandal is the *hammam* or the bath and to the south of the path leading to the Masjid is a 22 metre-deep *baoli*.

It is believed that Sher Shah left the Purana Qila unfinished, and it was completed by Humayun after he recaptured the throne of Delhi.

In front of the Purana Qila, on the opposite side of the road is Khairul Manazil Masjid built in 1561. An inscription over the central arch of the prayer chamber says that it was erected by Maham Anga, during the reign of Emperor Akbar. Maham Anga was a wet nurse of Akbar, and the mother of Adham Khan, whose tomb in Mehrauli is locally called the Bhul-Bhulaiyan.

Next to Khairul Manazil Masjid is the imposing Sher Shah Gate, believed to have been the southern gateway of Sher Shah's city, Shergarh. Built with red sandstone it is also called Lal Darwaza or red gate.

Another gate to Sher Shah's extensive city is said to be Khuni Darwaza, now on Bahadur Shah Zafar Marg. Believed to be Shergarh's north gate, it was here that two sons and a grandson of the last Mughal emperor, Bahadur Shah II were put to death by the British after the Uprising of 1857. Their bodies were displayed here and local folklore has it that their blood still drips from the ceiling of the gateway.

Sher Shah

The family of Sher Shah Sur, born Farid, came from Roh in the Sulaiman Range in modern Afghanistan. His grandfather Ibrahim was a horse trader who switched to soldiering after migrating to India during the reign of Bahlol Lodi and gradually rose to secure himself a *jagir* near Narnaul.

Ibrahim's son, Hasan, shifted east and got a bigger *jagir* near Sasaram in southern Bihar. Hasan's son, Farid was a headstrong young man and his frequent clashes with his father led to his moving on to Jaunpur, a great centre of scholarship. He studied diligently there and according to some accounts was even employed in the provincial administration in a minor capacity. His father, seeing his potential, called him back and handed over the administration of his *jagir* to him.

Farid managed the estate with an efficiency that bordered on the ruthless. Yet he was just, and soon tamed the lawlessness rampant in the area. According to Abbas Khan Sarwani, who chronicled his doings in the *Tuzuk-i-Sher Shahi*, 'If any soldier or peasant had a complaint, Farid would examine it in person, and carefully investigate the cause, nor did he ever give way to carelessness or sloth'.

But he was relieved of his duties when his father, giving in to a

Below left:
Sher Shah Gate or Lal Darwaza believed to have been the south gate to Sher Shah's citadel, Shergarh

Below right:
Talaqi Darwaza

concubine's pressure, took away the administration of the *jagir* from him. Farid lobbied with the then sultan, Ibrahim Lodi, for redress but to no avail. It was only on his father's death that Farid was able to secure a *firman* from the Lodi king making over Sasaram to him.

By now rechristened Sher Khan for having killed a tiger single-handed, he also consolidated his personal worth by marrying two rich widows – one brought him the strategically-located fort of Chunar and the other, untold riches.

Gradually, Sher Khan rose to became the *de facto* ruler of Bihar, but continued to read the *khutba* in the name of the Mughal emperor.

Only when he started extending his influence eastward and overran Bengal – still technically on the emperor's behalf – did Humayun set off to subdue him in 1537. The two tarried for another two years before open battle ensued at Chausa in 1539, where Humayun was forced to beat an undignified retreat, and was reduced to crossing the Ganga to safety on an inflated water-bag supplied by a *bhishti*.

Sher Khan then returned to Gaur and was crowned Sher Shah, and assumed the title of *Sultan-ul-Adil* or the Just Ruler. It was only after this that he began his march on to Agra, the seat of the Mughal empire. Humayun finally sallied forth to meet him and the armies clashed at Kannauj on May 17, 1540, where the Mughals were thoroughly and absolutely routed.

Sher Shah proved to be an extremely competent ruler, forging a cohesive kingdom out of administrative chaos. Beginning with Bengal, he divided a province into *sarkars* or districts, each under the parallel control of a military administrator and a revenue officer. This structure was repeated in the *parganas* or sub-districts. Also, all provincial officers were posted out after two years to prevent any of them from developing a stake in the areas under their control. He built roads, caravansarais and *dak chaukis*, and generally laid the foundations of an administrative system that was later adopted by both the Mughals and the British.

Sher Shah had a burning desire to build monuments 'with such embellishments that friend and foe might render their tribute of applause and that my name might remain honoured upon earth until the day of resurrection'. This wish, however, remained unfulfilled. All he could accomplish was the rudiments of a city built on Humayun's Dinpanah (Purana Qila) in Delhi, besides, of course, his mausoleum at Sasaram in Bihar.

His lasting regret in this matter has also been recorded, 'None of these aspirations has God allowed me to carry into effect, and I shall carry my regrets with me to my grave.'

Sher Shah died as he had lived – striving for victory. In 1545, during the siege of Kalinjar, a rocket fired at that fort ricochetted back and exploded in the Sur camp. Sher Shah suffered severe burns. Although, says Badauni, his physicians poured quantities of sandalwood paste and rosewater over him, his body let off a 'scorching heat, whose intensity increased hour by hour'. Sher Shah held out for several hours, until the fort gave in. Then, giving praise to the Lord for his final victory, he died.

Below:
Sher Mandal, the pavilion built by Sher Shah, is famous as the place where Emperor Humayun fell to his death

Humayun's Tomb

*T*he life of Humayun, the second Mughal emperor, was marked by struggle and vicissitude. He ascended the throne of Delhi after the death of his father, Babur, in 1530. The Mughal empire was not yet firm on its foundations, and Humayun had to suppress a number of rebellions at the outset of his reign. Early success was followed by prolonged disaster.

In 1539 Sher Khan, an Afghan nobleman who ruled over tracts of what is now Bihar and Bengal, rose victoriously against him and the vanquished emperor fled the country. He spent 15 years in exile, some of them at the court of Shah Tahmasp of Persia, and in 1555 returned with a borrowed Persian army, recovered his lost dominion and re-established the Mughal Empire. He did not long survive his return and died on January 19, 1556, after a fall on the steps of his library in Sher Mandal, a monument inside what is today called Purana Qila.

Humayun was buried in Purana Qila, but, according to some scholars, the emperor's remains were removed from there to a *supurdgah* or temporary tomb in Sirhind when Hemu advanced upon Delhi in 1556 and the Mughals had to vacate the city. He was re-buried in the Sher Mandal again when Akbar defeated Hemu, and was moved into the mausoleum erected in 1569 by his widow, Haji Begum, also known as Bega Begum, at an estimated cost of rupees fifteen lakhs.

Scholars have disagreed over the date of construction. Sayyid Ahmad Khan in his book *Asarus-Sanadid* (1846), Part III, p.56, gives the date of its construction as AH 973 (AD 1565) and this date has been followed by all later writers. But an older manuscript of the Siyarul Manazil by Sangin Beg (late 18th century), at present in Delhi's Red Fort Museum, states that the foundation of the tomb was laid in the 14th year of Akbar's reign, that is, 1569.

Site Map of Humayun's Tomb Complex

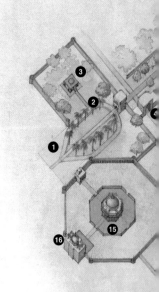

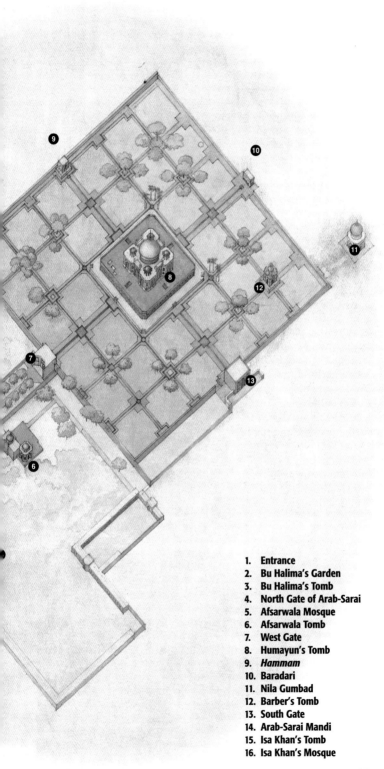

1. Entrance
2. Bu Halima's Garden
3. Bu Halima's Tomb
4. North Gate of Arab-Sarai
5. Afsarwala Mosque
6. Afsarwala Tomb
7. West Gate
8. Humayun's Tomb
9. *Hammam*
10. Baradari
11. Nila Gumbad
12. Barber's Tomb
13. South Gate
14. Arab-Sarai Mandi
15. Isa Khan's Tomb
16. Isa Khan's Mosque

A radially symmetrical plan, a garden setting and a bulbous double dome on an elongated drum are the main features of Humayun's Tomb. Each of these had strong Timurid associations for the Mughals, who gloried in their dynastic descent from Timur.

Most 15th century Timurid architecture was built to symmetrical plans. These included monuments such as the Ghur-i-Mir (1404) built by Timur for his grandson at Samarkand, and which was his own final resting place as well; Ishrat Khaneh also at Samarkand (c.1460-64); and the shrine of Abu Nasr Parsa in Balkh (c.1460-64). The Ghur-i-Mir also had a bulbous dome and high drum that was repeated in Humayun's Tomb, the first mausoleum for an emperor of the Mughal dynasty.

As one of the first important buildings the Mughals erected in India, Humayun's Tomb introduced purely Persian features to the subcontinent, but it also drew several elements from the land it was built in. The red sandstone and white marble, for instance, was a common feature of 14th century architecture of the Delhi Sultanate.

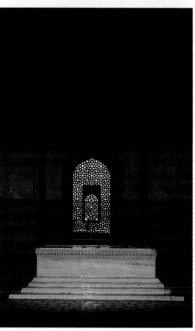

Above:
The south-west face of the mausoleum

Left:
The emperor's cenotaph

Humayun's Tomb – ground plan

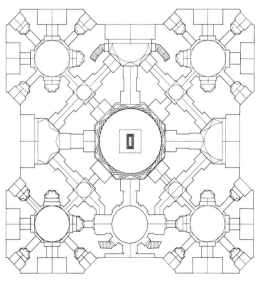

Based on Ebba Koch, *Mughal Architecture*, Delhi, 2002

Red Sandstone and White Marble

*I*ndo-Islamic builders have favoured this architectural scheme ever since it made its first appearance in the Alai Darwaza added to the Quwwat-ul-Islam Mosque by Alauddin Khalji in 1311. It remained prominent through the Delhi Sultanate until Ghiyasuddin Tughluq's Tomb was built around 1325. The medium is then eclipsed for the better part of the 15th century and is seen again only in the Lodi period Moth ki Masjid (*c*.1488-1517).

Under the highly aesthetic Mughals, the combination again becomes the standard means of finishing a building. The mosque of Jamali-Kamali (*c*.1528-29), the Qala-i-Kuhna Masjid (*c*. 1534), and the tomb of Ataga Khan (*c*.1566-67) are early Mughal monuments in Delhi that use the scheme.

Right:
A subsidiary arch on the west face of Humayun's Tomb

The symbolic qualities of Humayun's Tomb reflect a bold attempt to create an architecture that grows out of, but is distinct from, earlier Islamic buildings in India and Iran, the two poles of the Mughal world.

– Glenn D Lowry, 1987

The mausoleum of Humayun and the enclosure-walls are built of three kinds of stone. The walls and the two gateways are of local quartzite with red sandstone dressing and marble inlay. The red sandstone for the main building came from Tantpur near Agra and was used with white marble from Makrana in Rajasthan.

In the centre of the garden, the mausoleum itself rises from a wide and lofty platform about 6.5 metres high, which in turn stands upon a podium just over a metre high. The latter is the only feature of the mausoleum built of quartzite, the remainder being entirely of red or yellowish sandstone with marble panels or outlines and a marble-covered dome. Each side of the high terrace is pierced by 17 arches, while the corners of the structure are chamferred, giving the monument a pleasing depth. At each corner, an oblique arch cuts the angle.

The central arch on each side opens on to an ascending staircase. To the east of the southern stair a horizontal passage leads to the actual tomb below the monument. The remaining arches open into cells, most of which contain subsequent and subsidiary tombs. The floor of the terrace is paved with red sandstone and contains a number of unidentified graves.

Inside, the octagonal tomb chamber rises through two storeys and is surrounded by smaller octagonal chambers at the diagonal points. These chambers also house a number of other tombstones, making Humayun's mausoleum almost a family one.

Family Tomb

*N*o other mausoleum contains so many distinguished dead of the Mughal dynasty as the mausoleum of Humayun. Although his three immediate successors were buried elsewhere, most of the later emperors, princes and princesses as well as their attendants lie buried close to him. The identification of individual graves is uncertain, since all are uninscribed.

It is said that in the subsidiary chambers of the mausoleum are interred Humayun's two wives, Haji Begum, who initiated the building of her husband's tomb and Hamida Banu Begum, Akbar's mother. The headless body of Dara Shikoh, the unfortunate son of Shahjahan who was murdered by the ruthless Aurangzeb and a string of later Mughal emperors including Jahandar Shah, Farukkhsiyar and Alamgir II are also buried here.

Subsidiary tomb chamber to the north-west of the main tomb chamber

The central hall containing the cenotaph (vertically above the actual tomb in the basement) is roofed by a double dome carried on squinches, with plastered interlace in the spandrels. It is in three stages, of which the central is a gallery and the uppermost a clerestory. Most of the openings are filled with sandstone grilles.

Mirak Mirza Ghiyas

*H*umayun's Tomb is said to have been built under the supervision of Mirak Mirza Ghiyas, an architect of Persian descent. It is said that Haji Begum was greatly taken with the Persian style of building and commissioned Ghiyas precisely because of his familiarity with the architecture of that region. And the Persian builder, who had worked extensively in Herat and Bukhara, gave India its first dome in the Persian tradition.

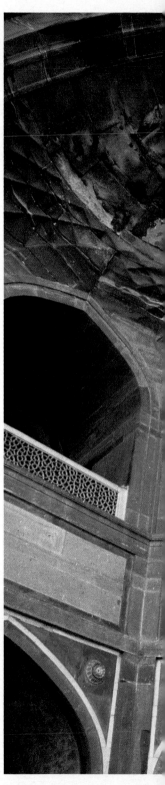

Right:
Details of the eastern archway of Humayun's Tomb

Between each of the octagonal wings on the diagonal sides of the central tomb lie the great arched lobbies that dominate the exterior elevation. Although varied in terms of their numerous panels and recesses, these conform essentially to the three-fold scheme characteristic of Persian architecture, the great central arches being flanked by a smaller but emphatic arch in each wing.

Left:
Details of ornamental brackets of pavilions on the terrace of Humayun's Tomb

Humayun's Tomb – sectional elevation

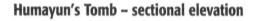

Humayun's Tomb was among the first structures in India to use a double dome. This device, a favourite of Persian builders, gave a building an imposing exterior height but kept the ceiling of the central hall in proportion with the interior heights.

The dome is also remarkable in that it is the first major full dome to be seen in India. Earlier domes were not full in the sense that their shape never traced a full semi-circle.

The outer dome of Humayun's Tomb is covered with marble and is bulbous in shape. It is supported by pavilions or *chhattris* above the wings and portals. These, historians believe, served as a *madrasa* or college in the days when the tomb was a living monument. The *chhattris* serve the added purpose of masking the drum from view. These pavilions, augmented by carefully graded pinnacles at all angles of the building, unite the soaring outline of the dome with the horizontal lines of the main structure and give strength and coherence to the design.

Based on Ebba Koch, *Mughal Architecture*, Delhi, 2002

Domes

*I*ndian indigenous architecture was unacquainted with the dome until the advent of the Muslims. The roofs of Hindu temples were either flat-topped or modelled on mountain *sikharas* to meet in a peak above the *sanctum sanctorum*.

Muslim builders, on the other hand, had long been accustomed to arcuate construction and used squinches to raise domes above their buildings.

When the Islamic forces overran north India in the 13th century, the Muslim rulers were keen to replicate their domed buildings here. But, the local workmen were unfamiliar with the technique of raising domes and the earliest domes constructed by them, like the one that covered Iltutmish's Tomb (1235) in the Qutb Complex, were amateur efforts and soon caved in.

When the local builders finally mastered the art of constructing domes, they built them as half domes, that

Alai Darwaza, 1311

Ghiyasuddin Tughluq's Tomb, 1321-1325

Bara Gumbad, Lodi Garden, 1484

is, domes that did not sketch a complete semi-circle. In fact, most Indo-Islamic monuments until the 15th century had half domes raised above them and it is only with the buildings of the Lodi dynasty (1451-1526) that the domes began to curve a full semi-circle.

The rounded shape of the early Indo-Islamic dome differed greatly from Persian domes, which were bulbous semi-circles rising from a high drum. The first time this Persian-style dome appeared on the Indian skyline was in Humayun's Tomb.

The dome of Humayun's mausoleum is significant on another count – it is the first major double dome to be constructed in India. A double dome is one composed of two shells, with a gap between the two layers. The outer shell provides the elevated dome imposing height while the considerably lower inner shell provides the central chamber a roof proportionate to its dimensions. This style of raising a dome had been prevalent in West Asia for a while before Mirak Mirza Ghiyas brought it to India.

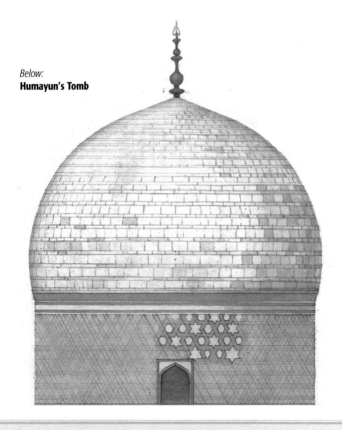

Below:
Humayun's Tomb

The walled enclosure of the tomb is entered through two gates. The main gate to the south, which is now closed, and a less imposing west gate. The south gate is a towering 15.5 metres high. It stands on a podium approached by a flight of five steps. The ground floor comprises a central hall, octagonal and domed, with rectangular wings. There are square and oblong rooms on the first floor of the gateway. The outer angles are adorned with octagonal pinnacles topped with a lotus design. The gate is flanked externally by screen-walls with arched recesses.

Adjoining the south gate is a compound on the west, 146 metres by 32 metres, built against the exterior face of the main enclosure-wall. It contains a low-roofed verandah, with 25 arched entrances and was possibly meant to accommodate the many attendants of the royal tomb. Its main exit is towards the south, but it is also connected with the tomb by a small doorway. There is another dilapidated building flanking the eastern side of the gate externally.

Above:
Details of the bloomed lotus on a minaret

Left:
The imposing western arch

Both this building and the verandah are later additions.

The west gate, by which visitors now enter the tomb-enclosure, also stands on a podium with five steps and is two storeys high. It consists of a 7 metre-square central hall, with square side-rooms on the ground floor, and oblong rooms on the first. It is approached from the front and back through portals 10.7 metres high. The gate is flanked externally with arched recesses and measures 15 metres from the floor-level to the parapet. It is surmounted at the outer angles by small *chhattri* pavilions, 1.5 metres square.

The northern, southern and western walls of the enclosure are of

Above:
The domed ceiling of the southern or main entrance to the tomb chamber

plastered rubble and are 5.8 metres high. The interior face contains recessed arches with pointed heads and the outer face is crowned with merlons in relief.

On the east or the river side, the enclosure-wall is just about 1.5 metres in height, except for some 64 metres towards the south end, where it is again 5.8 metres high. Only this portion of the eastern wall is plastered, and it contains recessed arches on both faces. The lower wall was doubtless meant to afford an open view of the river Yamuna from the tomb and the garden. The enclosure-walls were built in several stages, as is indicated by breaks in the bond.

Humayun in Exile

Losing his kingdom at Kannauj in 1540, Humayun fled Agra with his family and treasure. He drifted through Sind and Rajasthan, wandering from fort to fort and kingdom to kingdom in search of refuge and support to take on Sher Shah again. But, neither the King of Sind, nor sundry Rajput *rajas* offered him concrete help to regain his lost dominions and Humayun decided finally to flee Hindustan.

The only bright spot in this meander through desert lands was the fact that on October 15, 1542, Humayun's young bride, Hamida Banu Begum, gave birth to a son in Umarkot. He was named Jalaluddin Muhammad Akbar. When he received the happy news, Humayun broke a pod of musk and handed out the fragrant pieces to his men, with a wish that the little boy's 'fame will, I trust, be one day expanded all over the world, as the perfume of the musk now fills the apartment'.

In 1543, accompanied by Hamida and a band of men dwindled to 40, the emperor without a kingdom crossed the Indus and climbed into the mountains of Afghanistan. Repulsed by his half-brother Kamran, the ruler of Kandahar, he decided to cross the mountain passes into the safety of the Persian empire. It was bitterly cold and barren, and the party was ill-equipped for the march. Fortunately they had left the infant Akbar behind in Kandahar in Humayun's half-brother Askari's care.

Humayun's efficient general Bairam Khan had been sent on ahead to probe the mind of Shah Tahmasp I and had been assured that his master was welcome in Persia. So, by early 1544 Humayun crossed into Persian territory.

Shah Tahmasp's welcome was more than warm; it was meticulous. His letter to his provincial governor detailing the reception Humayun was to get on Persian soil was 14 pages long. The Shah's *firman* detailed every facet of the royal reception, from the 'coloured and smart' clothes the guard of honour was to wear, down to the specification that the bread to be laid before the hapless Mughal emperor was to be 'kneaded with milk and butter and seasoned with fennel seeds and poppy seeds'.

After his reception at the border, Humayun made his leisurely way to Kazvin, the Persian capital. It was when the two monarchs met here, that Humayun took out a green-flowered purse that he had been carrying in his tunic pocket for three years since he fled Agra. It contained a mother-of-pearl box which he gave to the Shah. Inside, nestled on a bed of precious gems, was a diamond that was to be famous in history as the Koh-i-noor.

The Shah entertained Humayun at his court for many months and then, after a lavish feast held in 300 tents to the accompaniment of 12 musical bands, offered him 12,000 horsemen and the wherewithal of war to help regain Hindustan. Humayun set off, but only after he had taken in a trip to the Caspian Sea and another to the wondrous city of Tabriz. It was well into 1545 before he advanced on Kandahar as his first stop to Hindustan.

Kandahar could not hold out for long and Humayun rode into the city in September 1545. That, in fact, was the turning point in Humayun's fortunes, for soon after he managed to capture Kabul. For the next seven years Humayun and his brother Kamran fought for ascendancy until Humayun triumphed.

Meanwhile in India, the death of Sher Shah's son, Islam Shah, in 1554 had plunged the newly-forged Sur empire into anarchy. And Bairam Khan, at the head of the Mughal army, marched right through the Punjab before he was even challenged. Finally, Sikandar Shah, the strongest of the three claimants to the Sur throne, took on the Mughal army at Sirhind in June 1555. Bairam Khan had a smaller army but subtler strategy helped him win India back for Humayun. A month later, Humayun was reinstated on the throne of Hindustan.

Towards the centre of the inner face of the north wall stands an arcaded pavilion on a platform 2.1 metres high. It contains an octagonal tank, about one metre across, and the room appears to have been a *hammam* or bath. It is plastered but undecorated. Behind this pavilion, on the north side of the enclosure-wall is a rubble-built circular well, which supplied water both to the bath and the channels of the *charbagh*.

The centre of the eastern wall has a more decorative pavilion, with a verandah along its east front, which faces the river. The details of the sandstone columns and elaborately cusped arches indicate that this pavilion is a later addition, probably of the 17th century.

Humayun's Tomb marked the end of the sombre style of early Indo-Islamic architecture and laid the foundation of the ornate style that characterised the mature Indo-Islamic architecture and culminated in the Taj. The rigid main lines of the building are diversified by *chhattris* or pavilions essentially Hindu in origin and, without impairing the strength of the design, give it a coherence foreign to its Persian prototypes.

Above:
Finial on top of the marble dome consisting of a series of copper vessels

Humayun's Tomb and the Uprising of 1857

*T*he final phase in the active history of the tomb was the capture here of the last Mughal emperor of Delhi, Bahadur Shah II, and the three princes Mirza Mughal, Mirza Khizar Sultan and Mirza Abu Bakr by Lieutenant Hodson during the 1857 Uprising. He rode through the portals of the mausoleum on September 22, 1857 and called upon the retainers of the princes to surrender their arms.

The Gardens of the Mughals

*T*he concept of paradise as a garden is one of mankind's oldest ideals. The image of a place of perfect eternal peace and plenty can probably help make a difficult temporal existence meaningful and its transitory nature acceptable. The paradise promised in the *Quran* consists of several terraces of gardens, each more splendid than the last.

The ancestor of the Mughals, Timur, took great pride in the gardens he built. Timur's gardens, within which were rich encampments decorated with plunder from captive nations and his throne over the watercourses representing the four rivers of life, became famous world-wide.

Babur, the first Mughal emperor, built many

innovative gardens, always with water. A layout for gardens, as described in his memoirs, set the design for all future Mughal gardens, known as the *charbagh* or 'four-folded garden'. The introduction of new materials might have changed appearances, but the basic design of Mughal gardens remained the same.

Below:
The garden in Humayun's Tomb with the west gate in the distance

On his death, Babur was first buried at a garden in Agra and later, in accordance with his expressed wish, was interred in a garden in Kabul with a simple marble cenotaph covering his body.

Babur introduced into India the Timurid-Persian scheme of a walled-in garden, subdivided into four quarters by raised walkways and canals. Art historian Ebba Koch writes that such a garden became the foundation stone for the development of Mughal Agra as a riverbank city with a succession of walled gardens on both sides of the Yamuna.

Of Babur's gardens in India the rock-cut Bagh-i Nilufar (Lotus garden) at Dholpur (1526-29) is preserved to some extent. Its modest structures are far less than what one would expect from the emperor's descriptions in his memoirs, *Baburnama*. Of his *charbagh* or Bagh-i Hasht Bihisht (Garden of the Eight Paradises) in Agra nothing much remains. According to a recently discovered 18th century plan of Agra at the Jaipur Palace Museum, the garden was situated on the other side of Yamuna adjoining the Mahtab Bagh and almost opposite the later Taj Mahal.

However, it is the later imperial tomb gardens, of which Humayun's Tomb is the first, that are considered the greatest innovation of the Mughals in garden architecture.

In all the great tomb gardens – Humayun's in Delhi, Akbar's in Sikandra, Jahangir's in Lahore, the Taj Mahal, the tomb of Itmad-ud-Daulah in Agra and the Bibi ka Maqbara in Aurangabad – the design of the tomb and garden were treated in unison. Each was meant to enhance the beauty of the other. Symbolically, these were the perfect embodiment of the Islamic ideal, the ultimate paradise garden, with the emperor forever in paradise. The large square enclosure, divided with geometric precision, was the ordered universe.

In the centre, the tomb itself rose like the cosmic mountain above four rivers represented by the water-channels. Eternal flowers, herbs, fruit, water, birds such as those of paradise added further character to the tomb garden.

Humayun's Tomb is the first preserved Mughal garden on a classical *charbagh* pattern. The paved walkways (*khiyabans*) that divide the garden into four parts terminate in gatehouses and subsidiary structures. With the tomb as its centrepiece, the garden enclosure occupies 30 acres. Enclosed within a 6-metre high arcaded wall on three sides, it is divided into quarters by causeways 14-metres wide. The causeways are provided with stone edging, with a narrow water channel flowing along the centre.

Each of the quadrants is further divided into eight plots with minor causeways. The intersections of these causeways are marked by rectangular or octagonal pools, that are occasionally foliated. Water entered the garden from the north pavilion, and also from the western side. Terracotta pipes fed the fountains and drained away excess water.

The tomb of Akbar in Sikandra (1613) outside Agra stands in the centre of a classical *charbagh* whose main walkways terminate in one real and three blind gates.

Jahangir spent a lot of energy laying out elaborate gardens, beginning with the garden at Verinag in Kashmir at the source of the Jhelum.

Jahangir's other garden projects include the famous Shalimar Bagh outside Srinagar where he built Farah Baksh (Joy-Imparting).

His son, Shahjahan added a *charbagh* named Fayz Baksh (Bounty-Bestowing), to the north-east of his father's Farah Baksh in 1634. Shalimar Bagh has two terraced *charbaghs* along a central waterway. Inspired by the Shalimar Bagh, Shahjahan went on to build a garden by the same name at Lahore.

The Nishat Bagh (Garden of Gladness) also situated on the bank of Dal Lake in Srinagar, was built by Shahjahan's father-in-law, Yasmin Daula Asaf Khan. Here the Mughal garden of Kashmir is given an unprecedented monumental scale by extending it to twelve terraces.

The tomb architecture of the Mughals culminates in the Taj Mahal. The tomb garden here forms part of a larger, carefully planned complex. In its layout the garden is a typical riverside garden on a monumental scale, with a raised terrace combined with a lower *charbagh*.

One of the best preserved examples of the late Mughal style at Delhi is the mausoleum of Safdarjung (1753-54). It is the last great mausoleum in the classical Mughal tradition of a nine-fold plan set on a podium in the centre of a four-parterre *charbagh* garden.

Left:
One of the last great Mughal gardens built on the *charbagh* plan is in Safdarjung's Tomb in Delhi

Revitalisation of Humayun's Tomb Gardens

The Archaeological Survey of India in collaboration with the Aga Khan Trust for Culture and under the aegis of the National Culture Fund is engaged in a major project to revitalise the gardens of Humayun's Tomb.

Up to early 2003, development activities will be carried out within the tomb-enclosure in order to revive the gardens and associated water systems. All intervention will be based on research on the site itself, other Mughal gardens and a minimalist approach to restoration.

The Oberoi Hotels group has sponsored a carefully designed lighting system to illuminate the tomb and enhance its impact on the city's skyline. The lighting simulates the moonlight effect. Light fixtures have been kept over 100 metres from the tomb and the cables placed underground so as not to disturb the visual appeal of the monument.

Work began in March 2001 and over 3,000 truck-loads of earth have already been removed from the garden and over 3 kms of pathway edging-stones have been reset in order to restore the garden-pathway relationship. Also, over 40 sandstone benches of a design first used in the garden in 1917 have been provided.

In order to eliminate standing water during the monsoons and recharge ground water, 128 recharge pits have been dug and two 8-metre diameter wells in the eastern portion of the garden have been cleared of rubble and excavated to a depth of 15 metres.

The water channels will be repaired and the system partially restored for flowing water. The conservation approach adopted, coupled with the need to conserve water will mean that not all portions of the system will have flowing water. In any case there is no historical evidence that the system was ever used in this manner.

The proposed planting scheme for the garden is based on an interpretation of Mughal texts. The peripheral pathway is to be planted with trees such as mango, said to have been favoured by the Mughals. It has been recorded that oranges and lemons were planted at the tomb since Humayun had a liking for these fruits, and these will be planted here again. Sweet-smelling and flowering shrubs recorded in Mughal texts will also be planted.

Conservation work will also be undertaken on minor structures in the garden and the site shall be made completely accessible for wheel-chair users.

Other Monuments in Humayun's Tomb Complex

*T*he emperor's mausoleum stands in the middle of a large square garden (*charbagh*), screened by high walls with gateways to the south and west. In the south-east corner of the garden is a picturesque tomb of red sandstone, known as the Barber's Tomb, and Nila Gumbad is in the same direction.

Outside the north-east corner of the enclosure of Humayun's mausoleum are the remains of a house in the severe 14th century Tughluq style, which according to tradition was the residence of Hazrat Nizamuddin Aulia, who died in 1325. The other monuments within the complex include Afsarwala mosque and tomb, Arab-Sarai, Bu Halima's Garden, and the tomb and mosque of Isa Khan.

Barber's Tomb

The figure 999 carved on one of the graves inside the monument is the only clue to the date of this monument. The figure, it is assumed, stands for the Hijra date corresponding to 1590-91, a date consistent with the architectural style of the building. No one knows who is buried in this picturesque tomb of red and grey sandstone, locally known as the Barber's Tomb (Nai ka Gumbad). Historians conjecture that it was built for the emperor's favourite *nai* (barber).

The tomb stands on a podium 2.44 metres high and 24.3 metres square, reached by seven steps from the south. The building is square on plan and consists of a single compartment covered with a double dome. The inner dome is of unusual design and consists of a small central cupola carried on four intersecting

and arched ribs.
The two marble graves
inside are inscribed
with verses from the
Quran. Outside there
is a portal-arch
7 metres high on each
side. The outer dome
which is shouldered,
rises from a 16-sided
drum and is crowned
by an inverted lotus
finial-base, though the
finial is now missing.
At each corner of the
main structure is a
pavilion (*chhattri*), that
still retains the remains
of blue, green and
yellow tile inlay.

As it happens,
this is not the
only monument in
Delhi to honour a
nai. There is a small
ruined fortress
named Nai ka Kot
about ten minutes
drive from
Tughluqabad Fort.
No one really knows
why it is called Nai
ka Kot (barber's
fort) or who this
influential 14th
century barber was.
Historians believe
that the fort was
built by Muhammad
bin Tughluq, while
he was supervising
the construction of
Adilabad Fort.

Below left:
Barber's Tomb

Below:
The *mihrab* inside

Nila Gumbad

Fifty yards outside the eastern wall of the enclosure of Humayun's mausoleum, on the south-eastern side is an impressive tomb of plastered stone covered with a blue dome commonly called the Nila Gumbad (Blue Dome).

According to archaeologist S A A Naqvi, the building probably existed even before Humayun's Tomb. He bases his conjecture on the fact that the outer face of the enclosure-wall of Humayun's Tomb, immediately opposite the Nila Gumbad, contains recessed arches which contrast with the plain construction of the wall everywhere else on this side; it also contains a doorway leading to the Nila Gumbad. These features indicate that the Gumbad already existed before, or was simultaneously designed with the enclosure-wall. It cannot therefore have been erected to enshrine the remains of a nobleman in Jahangir's court.

Unfortunately this monument is virtually inaccessible, as it has been encroached upon by families who live within its precincts.

Sayyid Ahmad Khan, in *Asarus-Sanadid* (1846) believed that it contained the remains of Fahim Khan, a faithful attendant of Abdur Rahim Khan who died in 1626 during the reign of Emperor Jahangir.

The building is mainly of local grey quartzite and is plastered both internally and externally. The dome is covered with dark blue tiles, and there are blue and yellow tiles round the drum. The tomb, octagonal on plan, stands on a platform 33.2 metres square and 1.5 metres high. The dome is raised on a high circular drum, and is crowned externally by an inverted lotus with a red sandstone finial. Inside it is carried on squinches with plastered interface and has a circular central panel profusely decorated with painted and incised plaster in Persian style. There is no monument over the grave. Externally the sides of the octagon contain four-centred recessed arches, of which those in the cardinal sides are pierced by square-headed doorways surmounted by four-centred and pierced tympana. The parapet is simple and without the usual pinnacles at the corners.

Chillah Nizamuddin Aulia

Outside the north-eastern corner of the enclosure of Humayun's mausoleum are the remains of a house in the Tughluq style. Though there is no historical reference available to substantiate the fact, it is believed to be the residence of Shaikh Nizamuddin Auliya (died in 1325), whose *dargah* is also close by. The austere form of architecture of the building is also consistent with a 14th century date.

The house stands on a platform 3.6 metres above the ground, and once faced the river Yamuna, which used to flow past the site. It consists of a low *dalan* (rear-chamber) behind a simple verandah with

*B*oth the Nila Gumbad and Sabz Burj now have blue domes, though the latter was once green in colour, as is evident from the few original tiles still left.

battered walls which opens towards the east. Remains of another room with massive walls and square headed doorways stand immediately to the south-east of the *dalan*. The eastern adjacent room is an addition, designed to fill the gap between the room mentioned above and the house to be described below.

Close to the *dalan* and adjoining the north-east corner of the enclosure of Humayun's mausoleum are the remains of another double-storeyed house with a verandah on its eastern front which once faced the river. The details of the red sandstone columns and lintels supported on brackets indicate that this was a construction of the Humayun-Akbar period. The house stands structurally independent of Humayun's Tomb.

Afsarwala Mosque

The mosque sits on a raised platform about 91 metres to the south-west of the west gate of Humayun's Tomb. The date of construction of this mosque is not known, although archaeological evidence places it between 1560 and 1567.

The building is of local quartzite with red sandstone dressing. It consists of a single, rather dilapidated, prayer-chamber divided into three bays, the central bay roofed by a dome carried on squinches. The inside of the central dome contains a painted circular panel. The central bay opens through a four-centred arch and is larger and higher than the flanking bays, which are also entered through four centred arches. The design conforms essentially to the 'triple *iwan*' of Persia.

The outer angles of the parapet are furnished with pinnacles, and the shouldered dome rises from a circular drum. S A A Naqvi writing in 1947 mentions unidentified graves in the courtyard of the mosque, but these must have been done away with and are no longer to be seen.

Afsarwala Tomb

On the same platform as the Afsarwala Mosque is an unidentified tomb that is locally known as Afsarwala Tomb. On one of the marble graves are inscribed quotations from the *Quran* and the number 974, which probably refers to the date in the Hijra era corresponding to AD 1566-67. The tomb dates to 1566-67 or a few years earlier.

Afsarwala Tomb is built with local grey quartzite with main lines of red sandstone and marble inlay. It consists of a single compartment, cruciform in plan internally, which is covered with a double dome. Externally the tomb is octagonal on plan: the sides of the octagon contain deeply recessed arches with square-headed doorways opening into the tomb-chamber in the four cardinal directions. The spandrels of the arches are decorated with round bosses of red sandstone. The outer dome rises from a high octagonal drum and is crowned by an inverted lotus finial-base bearing a red sandstone finial.

Both the mosque and the tomb are in honour of an *afsar*, however the identity of the *afsar* or officer who raised the buildings is not known. The Afsarwala Tomb has a grave with the date 974 marked on it, that corresponds to 1566-67, and according to archaeologists both the tomb and the mosque were built around this time.

Arab-Sarai

Haji Begum, Emperor Humayun's widow built the Arab-Sarai in 1560-61 to house the three hundred Arab *mullas* (priests), she is said to have brought with her from her pilgrimage to Mecca. However, archaeologist Y D Sharma may be right when he says 'Arab-Sarai is probably a misnomer, and the enclosure probably housed Persian, not Arab workers and craftsmen who were engaged in building Humayun's Tomb.'

It is a big *sarai* (rest-house) containing arched cells against its enclosure-walls. Almost all the cells are now in a dilapidated condition. The only structure worthy of notice is the northern gate, which is seen by the visitor on his right while proceeding to the emperor's mausoleum after crossing Bu Halima's Garden. The gate stands 12.2 metres high from its plinth and is built of local quartzite with red sandstone dressings and marble inlay. The main gate-chamber is hexagonal and was covered with a dome, now collapsed, with plastered interlace. Above the main arch of the gateway is a balcony window supported by six carved brackets, and on each side at the same level are more balcony windows with pyramidal domes enriched by yellow and blue tiles.

Arab-Sarai has two other gateways from the east and the west respectively. According to an inscription on the eastern gateway, that is close to the south-west corner of Humayun's mausoleum, it was actually the entrance to a *mandi* (market), added to it by one Mihr Banu during the reign of Jahangir. The market consisted of a series of arched rooms, now in ruins.

Below:
A view of the Arab-Sarai gate from behind Afsarwala Mosque

Garden of Bu Halima

As one approaches Humayun's Tomb from Mathura Road, one passes through a rectangular enclosure with a tomb in its northern half and a gateway on its east. This is the entrance of Bu Halima's Garden.

Nothing is known about Bu Halima and the origin of the garden locally named after the lady but architecturally the enclosure-walls and the gateway of the garden belong to the early Mughal period (16th century). It was certainly built earlier than the Arab-Sarai, the northern wall of which

abuts on the plastered exterior of the eastern garden-enclosure.

The garden is enclosed by rubble walls of local quartzite. Its eastern gateway is a simple structure consisting of an oblong main gate-chamber with octagonal wings.

Below:

Bu Halima's Garden, with what is believed to be her grave on the far right

The central portion of the eastern gateway of Bu Halima's Garden contains an ornamental arched recess, enclosing an arched doorway and a superimposed balcony-window supported by four brackets. The facade was once decorated with brilliant coloured tiles, very little of which are still extant. As in other monuments in the Humayun's Tomb complex, very little of the tile inlay work has survived the ravages of time and mankind.

At the north-east and north-west corners of the enclosure-walls are octagonal bastions, surmounted by small domed *chhattris* with glazed tile work. The dilapidated structure in the north corner of the garden enclosure is said locally to contain the grave of Bu Halima.

Above:
A detail from the outer face of the east gateway to Bu Halima's Garden

Left:
Inside the east gateway

It is only on nearing the Tomb of Humayun that one becomes aware of the strange and infinite number of ruined sepulchres all over the land.... Some of these are most exquisite as to architecture and finished ornament, and some of great interest....

– Edward Lear, 1874

Below:
Bu Halima's Garden beyond the gate of Isa Khan's Mosque and Tomb

Tomb and Mosque of Isa Khan

The tomb and mosque of Isa Khan Niyazi stand immediately to the south of Bu Halima's Garden. The Persian inscription on a red sandstone slab over the *mihrab* inside the tomb gives the tomb its identity:

'This tomb, which is an asylum of paradise, was built during the reign of Islam Shah, son of Sher Shah, may God perpetuate his kingdom and sovereignty, by Masnad Ali Isa Khan, son of Niyaz Aghwan, the chief chamberlain, in the Hijra year 954 (AD 1547- 48).'

Isa Khan's Tomb is built mainly of local grey quartzite with ornamental use of red sandstone. The rough masonry is covered with stucco plaster, and glazed tiles of different colours have been used in decorating the walls.

The tomb stands in the centre of an octagonal enclosure, the walls of which are crowned with plain battlements and the angles provided with circular bastions, giving it an air of strength. It is entered from the north through a gateway that stands on a podium approached by a flight of five steps. The main gate is in a dilapidated condition and the main gate chamber has collapsed. The square-headed doorway is of Hindu design.

The tomb is further enclosed by an inner low octagonal wall and is itself octagonal on plan. It stands on a podium just over one metre high. The square headed doorways on all sides of the tomb chamber except the south and the west are enclosed with *jalis* within recesses having four-centred arches.

Below:
Isa Khan's Tomb

Left:
Detail from inside Isa Khan's Tomb

Above:
Isa Khan's Mosque

The western side of the tomb is occupied by a four-centred *mihrab*, bordered by quotations from the *Quran*, while the southern side contains the entrance to the tomb-chamber. The medallion in the centre of the dome is enriched with painted floral decoration in Persian style, fringed by a quotation from the *Quran*.

Inside the tomb chamber there are two large graves and four smaller ones. The monument over the grave of Isa Khan, one of the two larger ones, is of marble and red sandstone. The floor is paved with sandstone slabs.

The main tomb chamber is surrounded by an arcaded verandah having three stilted, four-centred arches on each side of the octagon. The spandrels of the arches contain the remains of blue, green and yellow tile-inlay. It is crowned by a stone *chhajja*. The parapet above the verandah contains false merlons and from the eight angles rise slender pinnacles, topped with lotus-flower design. The squat dome springs from a 16-sided drum, the eight *chhattris* supported by columns of red sandstone rise from the roof level to surround the main dome and to harmonise the design.

The tomb of Isa Khan is similar on plan to those of Khan-i-Jahan Tilangani (died 1368-69), Mubarak Shah (died 1434), Mohammad

Shah (died about 1443) and Sikandar Shah Lodi (died 1517), all in Delhi. The tomb of Khan-i-Jahan Tilangani, in the village of Nizamuddin, is the earliest octagonal tombs to be found in the Delhi area. Persian influence can be seen in the octagonal tombs of 14th century Tughluq monuments, e.g., at Hauz Khas in Delhi.

The mosque of Isa Khan stands immediately to the west of the tomb inside the same enclosure-walls. It is a simple structure in contrast to the tomb. Built mainly of local grey quartzite, it is faced with red sandstone and is decorated with coloured tile inlay.

It stands on a platform almost a metre high and consists of a single prayer chamber that is divided into three bays. Internally the central dome is carried on squinches and the lateral domes rise from pendentives. The interior of the mosque is not elaborately decorated. The floor of the chamber is plastered.

Each bay is pierced by a four-centred arched entrance. The borders of the arches and the spandrels are decorated

Right:
Domed pavilion on the terrace of Isa Khan's Tomb

with blue and green tiles. The framework of the central arch is relieved at intervals by panels. A stone *chhajja* projects over the side bays. The parapet contains merlons in relief, and the corners of the central bay are decorated with pinnacles.

The central dome is high shouldered and springs from a 16-sided drum. The domed pavilions, supported by grey stone pillars, stand on either side of the central dome and retain the remains of blue tile inlay.

Below:
Isa Khan's Mosque

Right:
A detail of the left archway

Hazrat Nizamuddin

*A*bout 2 kms south of Purana Qila, on Mathura Road, is Hazrat Nizamuddin, one of the many historic village settlements that continues to exist within modern Delhi.

Nizamuddin gets its name from the Sufi saint, Shaikh Nizamuddin Auliya, who was born in Badaun in Uttar Pradesh in 1236, and lived most of his life in Delhi until his death in 1325. Among his illustrious disciples were the sultans, Alauddin Khalji and Muhammad bin Tughluq and Amir Khusro, one of India's most celebrated poets.

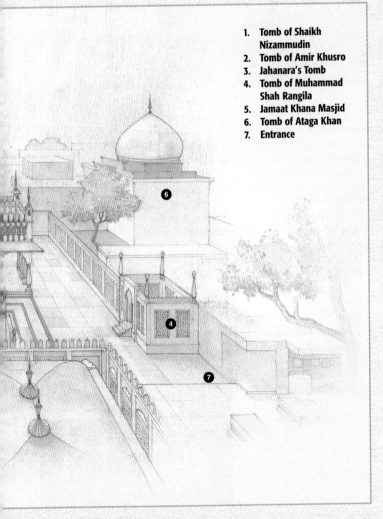

1. **Tomb of Shaikh Nizammudin**
2. **Tomb of Amir Khusro**
3. **Jahanara's Tomb**
4. **Tomb of Muhammad Shah Rangila**
5. **Jamaat Khana Masjid**
6. **Tomb of Ataga Khan**
7. **Entrance**

Left:
Sabz Burj

The entry point to Nizamuddin is marked by a traffic island with a blue-domed tomb known as **Sabz Burj** (*sabz*, green; *burj*, dome). The blue tiles are a recent restoration effort, but some of the original green, yellow and blue tiles can still be seen on the walls. It has high recessed arches on all sides and a high-drummed double dome covered with coloured tiles which gives it its name. Architecturally, the building probably belongs to the early Mughal period.
The British used this building as a police station for many years till the beginning of the last century.

The constant crowd of devotees outside **Nizamuddin's** *dargah* is testimony to the devotion that the saint still commands. Every Thursday, after sunset, *qawwals* sing the lyrics of Amir Khusro.

Shaikh Nizamuddin died in 1325, and his original tomb does not exist any longer.

Below:
Dargah
Nizamuddin

Faridun Khan, a nobleman, built the present structure in 1562-63 during the reign of Emperor Akbar.

The area around the tomb of the Shaikh has many big and small tombs that have been built over the centuries since it is considered auspicious to be buried near a saint's grave.

To the south of Nizamuddin's grave is the **Tomb of Amir Khusro**. Nearby are the marble screened tombs of Jahanara, the dutiful daughter of Emperor Shahjahan and the late Mughal emperor, Muhammad Shah Rangila (1719-48). Princess Jahanara's grave is covered with grass in accordance with the inscription on it, which says 'let naught cover my grave save the green grass: for grass well suffices as a covering for the grave of the lowly'.

At the northern gate of the *dargah* complex is a large *baoli*, the water of which is believed to have healing powers.

An interesting legend associated with the *dargah* is that of the skirmish between the saint and the first Tughluq king, Ghiyasuddin. Shaikh Nizamuddin was getting the *baoli* constructed at about the same time as the king was engaged in building his fortress at Tughluqabad. The king forbade his construction workers from working elsewhere, and so they decided to work for the Shaikh at night. This made Ghiyasuddin prohibit the sale of oil to Hazrat Nizamuddin, but the workers found that their lamps could be lit with the water of the *baoli*!

To the west of Shaikh Nizamuddin's tomb lies **Jamaat Khana Masjid**, veneered in red sandstone. It has three bays, each topped with a low dome. Its arches are fringed with lotus-bud decoration as in the arches of Alai Darwaza in the Qutb Complex. The mosque was built by a son of Sultan Alauddin Khalji, and is the oldest structure within the complex.

On the northern edge of Nizamuddin village outside the *dargah* complex, is **Ataga Khan's tomb**. It is an impressive structure in red sandstone thickly inlaid with marble and coloured tiles.

Sandwiched between two modern buildings, its original grandeur is still visible. Ataga Khan was the husband of Ji Ji Anga, Akbar's wet nurse, and held an important position in Akbar's court.

Above:
Chaunsath Khamba

In 1562 he was killed by Adham Khan, son of Maham Anga another wet nurse of Akbar. Adham Khan's tomb is in Mehrauli and is locally known as Bhul-Bhulaiyan.

The tomb of Mirza Aziz, Ataga Khan's son, built in 1623, is known as **Chaunsath Khamba**, because, as its name implies, it has sixty-four pillars supporting the roof. It is entered through a lofty, arched gateway adjacent to the **Ghalib Academy**.

In Nizamuddin West is also buried the famous 19th century Urdu poet, Mirza Ghalib. Mirza Ghalib's tomb, covered by a small marble structure, is kept locked within the precincts of the Ghalib Academy. The Ghalib Academy has a large library and an interesting museum which, besides some paintings, also has a large collection of rocks.

The **Tomb of Abdur Rahim Khan-i-Khanan**, is on the opposite side of Mathura Road. Abdur Rahim Khan, who died sometime in 1626-27, was the son of Bairam Khan, Akbar's loyal protector during his early years. An influential courtier in the courts of both Akbar and Jahangir, he was given the title of Khan-i-Khanan. Today Rahim is remembered as a popular Hindi poet.

The now completely dilapidated tomb was an architectural landmark in its time. Built of red sandstone, it followed the design of Humayun's Tomb and also had a marble dome. The dome was stripped of its marble slabs, which were later used on the dome of Safdarjung's Tomb.

Right:
The tomb of Abdur Rahim Khan-i-Khanan

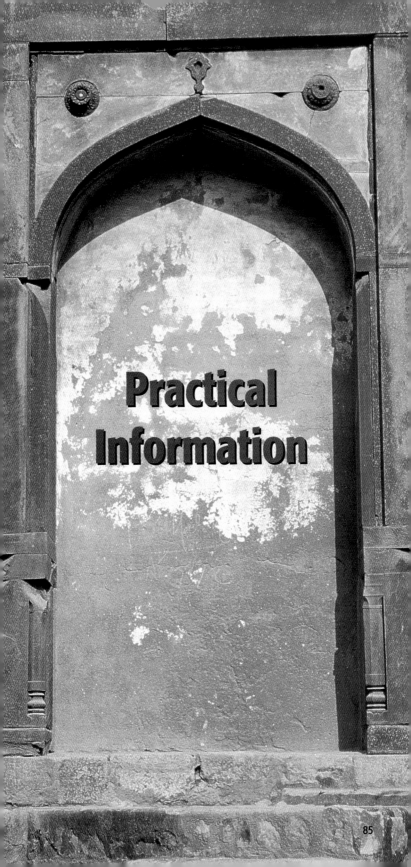

Practical
Information

PRACTICAL INFORMATION

Arriving in India

When to come to India

The best time to come to India is between October and March. During the winter months of December and January, the day temperature in the plains of North India is around 18°C (64°F) and could go down to 4°C (39°F) at night.

The summer months of May and June are hot, and the temperature can rise as high as 46°C (115°F). After the scorching heat, monsoons arrive towards the end of June and the rainy season stretches till September.

Before coming to India

There are a few things you need to take care of before travelling to India.

Visa

There are three kinds of visas for tourists.

1. **The 15-day single/double-entry transit visa.** This visa is valid for 30 days from the date of its issue.

2. **The 3-month multiple-entry visa.** This visa is valid for 90 days from the date of first entry into India, which must be within 30 days from the date of its issue.

3. **The 6-month multiple-entry visa.** This visa is valid for 180 days from the date of its issue, not from the date of entry into India.

Health

Your health during your travel in India depends on three things: Precautions taken before arrival, day-to-day health care, and efficiency in tackling emergencies

Precautionary medication is the best bet against common ailments like diarrhoea, dysentery and malaria. Malaria is a problem in India during the rainy season. So, if you are coming at that time of the year, do consult your doctor for precautionary anti-malarial medication. While in India, use mosquito repellent ointment.

If you are not already vaccinated against Hepatitis B, get it done before travelling.

Those not accustomed to Indian conditions are usually vulnerable to stomach problems. It is advisable to seek qualified medical advice before travelling and to carry your own first-aid kit.

Delhi has many government as well as privately run hospitals and nursing homes. The government hospitals have modern medical facilities but due to large patient turnout, medical assistance is slow.

Arriving in Delhi by Air

The Delhi airport is called the Indira Gandhi International Airport (IGI). It has two terminals: **Terminal 1** for domestic flights and **Terminal 2** for international ones. Terminal 2 is located about 19 kms from the city centre at Connaught Place and is equipped with all modern facilities; while

Terminal 1 is the old airport, basic but efficient. This is located 12 kms away from the city centre. The two terminals are 7 kms away from each other. There is a pre-paid taxi counter in the Arrival area of both Terminals. It is a good idea to hire a pre-paid taxi to avoid being over-charged.

Customs

There are two channels for customs clearance at international terminals in Indian airports: Green Channel and Red Channel.

Green Channel
This is for unhindered exit from the airport. You can walk through the Green Channel if you are not carrying goods that attract customs duty.

Red Channel
For those who have anything to declare, including money worth more than US $2,500.

Travel Within India

By Air

The biggest airline in India is Indian Airlines, the state-owned domestic carrier. Other major flyers are Jet Airways and Sahara India Airlines.

By Rail

Indian Railways runs a gigantic, modern and organised network that connects the metros to most major and minor destinations within India. However, trains in India are very crowded and it is necessary to reserve a seat or a berth to travel in any degree of comfort. Train tickets must be bought before you enter the train.

You will be penalised if you do not have one and intend to buy it on board.

Local Conveyance

 Taxis and auto-rickshaws are available in all cities, although only those in the metros are metered. In other places, it is best to fix the rate beforehand. And to bargain.

You can hire a private taxi for local and outstation tours at most hotels and airports. International car rental companies, as well as Indian private companies also run car-rental services. Most metros also have a dial-a-cab service. It is probably not a good idea to take a bus for local travel – especially if you have luggage.

Beware of pickpockets in buses. It is not advisable for women to travel alone in buses after 9 pm. Women should not wear tight clothes or mini skirts or shorts, especially while travelling in buses as they may attract lewd comments and worse.

Cycle-rickshaw

Cycle-rickshaws are a common sight in most parts of urban and rural India. They are a convenient means of covering short distances. Not only do they precariously balance two to three people, but often carry merchandise as well.

Car Rentals

There are several international and local companies that operate car rental services. Most car rentals accept international credit cards. Foreign nationals are usually required to pay in foreign exchange.

Another option is to engage the local white DLY taxi. These are available at all hotels and local taxi stands. The chauffeurs will always throw in a little extra insight while sightseeing and shopping, if you tip them well.

Guided Tours

There are full-day, guided city tour options on luxury coaches with qualified guides. The Delhi-New Delhi tours cover the city's major tourist spots: Lal Qila (Red Fort), Jama Masjid, Raj Ghat, Shanti Van, Qutb Minar, Jantar Mantar, Lotus Temple, India Gate, Rashtrapati Bhawan, Birla Mandir and Appu Ghar.

Tour operators

● Government of India Tourist Office
88 Janpath
Ph 3320005/3320008

(Pick-up points: 88 Janpath and Hotel Indraprastha)

● Ashok Tours & Travels (ITDC)
L 1 Connaught Place
Ph 3719039/3325035

(Pick-up points: L block and Hotel Indraprastha)

● Delhi Tourism (DTTDC)
Ph 3363607/3365358

(Pick-up point: Coffee Home, Baba Kharak Singh Marg).

Money

Indian Currency

Indian currency is called the Rupee. It is available in denominations of 1000, 500, 100, 50, 20, 10, 5, 2 , 1. One rupee equals 100 paise. Coins in common use are those of Rs 5, Rs 2 , Re 1 and 50 and 25 paise. The 20, 10 and 5 paise coins have

become redundant in big cities, but they still have value in smaller towns and in rural India. Be careful not to accept soiled notes.

Credit Cards

Credit cards are becoming increasingly popular in urban areas. All major international credit cards are used – Visa, Amex, Mastercard.

Banks

Banks are open from 10 am to 2 pm Monday to Friday and 10 am to 12 pm Saturdays. Banks are closed on Sundays and national holidays. Most international banks have several branches in Delhi.

Communications

Post Offices

 The main post offices in large towns provide a wide range of facilities, like telegraph, fax and a courier service that operates under the brand name EMS-Speed Post.

All Post Offices are open from 10 am to 6 pm Monday to Saturday.

Telephone

 ISD (international), STD (domestic long distance), and local telephone booths are available all over India. The rates for international calls are fixed, but calls within the country are charged on the basis of a pulse rate which varies for different cities, and for different times of the day. Most booths remain open till midnight. Some of these booths have facilities for sending and receiving fax messages.

PRACTICAL INFORMATION

Some Embassies & High Commissions in Delhi

Afghanistan
5/50 F Shanti Path
Chankyapuri
Ph 4103331
Fax 6875439

Argentina
B 2 Anand Niketan
Ph 4104846
Fax 4104864

Australia
1/50 G Shanti Path
Chanakyapuri
Ph 6888223/
6885556
Fax 6874126

Austria
EP 13 Chandragupta
Marg, Chanakyapuri
Ph 6889050/
6889049
Fax 6886929

Bangladesh
56 Ring Road
Lajpat Nagar III
Ph 6834668
Fax 6840596

Belgium
50 N Shanti Path
Chanakyapuri
Ph 6875728
Fax 6885821

Bhutan
Chandragupta Marg
Chanakyapuri
Ph 6889230
Fax 6876710

Canada
7/8 Shanti Path
Chanakyapuri
Ph 6876500
Fax 6876579

China
50 D Shanti Path
Chanakyapuri
Ph 6871586
Fax 6885486

Colombia
4/21 Shanti Path
Ph 6872771/ 6110773
Fax 6112486

Denmark
11 Aurangzeb Road
Ph 3010900
Fax 3792019

Finland
E 3 Nyaya Marg
Chanakaypuri
Ph 6115258
Fax 6886713

France
2/50 E Shanti Path
Chanakyapuri
Ph 6118790
Fax 6872305

Germany
6/50 G Shanti Path
Chanakyapuri
Ph 6871831
Fax 6877623

Greece
EP 32
Dr S Radhakrishnan
Marg, Chanakyapuri
Ph 6880700
Fax 6888010

Hungary
2/50 M Neeti Marg
Chanakyapuri
Ph 6114737
Fax 6886742

Indonesia
50 A Kautilya Marg
Chanakyapuri
Ph 6118642/6118646
Fax 6874402

Iran
5 Barakhamba Road
Ph 3329600
Fax 3354093

Ireland
230 Jor Bagh
Ph 4626714
Fax 4697053

Israel
3 Aurangzeb Road
Ph 3013238
Fax 3014298

Italy
50 E Chandragupta
Marg, Chanakyapuri
Ph 6114355

Japan
50 G Shanti Path
Chanakyapuri
Ph 6876581
Fax 6885587

Kenya
34 Paschimi Marg
Vasant Vihar
Ph 6146538
Fax 6146550

Kuwait
5A Shanti Path
Chanakyapuri
Ph 4100791
Fax 6873516

Malaysia
50 M Satya Marg
Chanakyapuri
Ph 6111291/6111292
Fax 6881538

Mongolia
34 Golf Links
Ph 4631728
Fax 4633240

Myanmar
3/50 F Nyaya Marg
Chanakyapuri
Ph 6889007
Fax 6877942

Mauritius
EP 41 Jesus & Mary
Marg, Chanakyapuri
Ph 4102161
Fax 4102194

Nepal
1 Barakhamba Road
Ph 3329218
Fax 3326857/
3329647

The Netherlands
6/50 F Shanti Path
Chanakyapuri
Ph 6884951
Fax 6884956

New Zealand
50 N Nyaya Marg
Chanakyapuri
Ph 6883170
Fax 6872317

Nigeria
21 Olof Palme Marg
Vasant Vihar
Ph 6146221
Fax 6146617

Norway
50 C Shanti Path
Chanakyapuri
Ph 6873573/
6873532
Fax 6873814

Pakistan
2/50 G Shanti Path
Chanakyapuri
Ph 6110601/6110605
Fax 6889200

Philippines
50 N Nyaya Marg
Chanakyapuri
Ph 6889091
Fax 6876401

Portugal
13 Sunder Nagar
Ph 4351262
Fax 4351252

Russia
Shanti Path
Chanakyapuri
Ph 6873800
Fax 6876823

Saudi Arabia
D 12 NDSE II
Ph 6256419/6252470
Fax 6259333

Singapore
E 6 Chandragupta
Marg, Chanakyapuri
Ph 6885659
Fax 6886798

South Africa
B 18 Vasant Marg
Vasant Vihar
Ph 6149411
Fax 6143605

South Korea
9 Chandragupta
Marg, Chanakyapuri
Ph 6885374/
6885375
Fax 6884840

Tourist Information Services

Spain
16 Sundar Nagar
Ph 4359004/
4359005
Fax 4359008

Sri Lanka
27 Kautilya Marg
Chanakyapuri
Ph 3010201
Fax 3793604

Sweden
Nyaya Marg
Chanakyapuri
Ph 4197100
Fax 6885401

Switzerland
Nyaya Marg
Chanakyapuri
Ph 6878372
Fax 6873093/
6112220

Thailand
56 N Nyaya Marg
Chanakyapuri
Ph 6118103
Fax 6872029

Turkey
50 N Nyaya Marg
Chanakyapuri
Ph 6889054
Fax 6881409

United Kingdom
Shanti Path
Chanakyapuri
Ph 6872161
Fax 6872882

**United States
of America**
Shanti Path
Chanakyapuri
Ph 4198000
Fax 4190017

Vietnam
17 Kautilya Marg
Chanakyapuri
Ph 3018059/
3012133
Fax 3017714

**Government of India
Tourist Office**
88 Janpath **Ph** 3320008

This is a reliable tourist
information centre. The staff is
helpful and the brochures and
maps useful. These introduce
the traveller to interesting places
for excursions, not only in and
around Delhi, but all over India.

**Delhi Tourism and
Transportation Development
Corporation (DTTDC)** has a
chain of offices all over Delhi.

Their central office is at
Bombay Life Building
N Block Middle Circle
Connaught Place
Ph 3730416/3315322
It is open from 7 am to 9 pm.

> It is advisable to go to an established travel agent to
> coordinate and organise your travel plans. The better known
> hotels have their own travel agents and tour operators.

State Information Centres

**Andaman and
Nicobar**
Andaman & Nicobar
Bhawan
12 Chanakyapuri
Ph 6871443

Andhra Pradesh
Andhra Bhawan
Ashoka Road
Ph 3382031

Assam
B 1 Baba Kharak
Singh Marg
Ph 3343961

Bihar
Kanishka Shopping
Plaza
Room No 216/217
19 Ashoka Road
Ph 3368371

Goa
18 Amrita Shergil
Marg
Ph 4629967

Gujarat
A 6 Baba Kharak
Singh Marg
Ph 3340305

Haryana
Chandralok Bldg,
36 Janpath
Ph 3324911

Himachal Pradesh
Chandralok Bldg
36 Janpath
Ph 3325320/
3324764

Jammu & Kashmir
Kanishka Shopping
Plaza,
Ashoka Road
Ph 3345373

Karnataka
6 Sardar Patel Marg
Kartaka Bhawan II
Chanakyapuri
Ph 4102263

Kerala
Kanishka Hotel
Shopping Plaza
Ashoka Road
Ph 3368541

Madhya Pradesh
204-205 Kanishka
Shopping Plaza,
Ashoka Road
Ph 3341187/3366528

Maharashtra
A 8 Baba Kharak
Singh Marg
Ph 3363773

Meghalaya
9 Aurangzeb Road
Ph 3014417

Orissa
B 4 Baba Kharak
Singh Marg
Ph 3364580

Rajasthan
Bikaner House
Near India Gate
Ph 3383837/
3386069

Sikkim
New Sikkim House,
14 Panchsheel Marg
Chanakyapuri
Ph 6115346

Uttar Pradesh
Chandralok Bldg
36 Janpath
Ph 3322251

West Bengal
A 2 Baba Kharak
Singh Marg
Ph 3373775

> **Email**
> Internet and
> email access are
> easily available.
> There are many
> cybercafes,
> where for a
> nominal amount
> you can access
> the Net.

PRACTICAL INFORMATION

Major International Airlines Offices

Air India
Upper GF
Jeevan Bharati Building
124 Connaught Circus
Ph 3731225
Fax 3739796
Airport Ph 5696621/5652050

Air France
7 Atma Ram Mansion
Scindia House
Connaught Place
Ph 3738004/3312853
Fax 3716259
Airport Ph 5652099/
5652294

Air Lanka
G 55 Connaught Circus
Ph 3731473-78
Fax 3731480
Airport Ph 5652957

Alitalia
2 H DCM Building
Barakhamba Road
Ph 3329551/3329556
Fax 3713699
Airport Ph 5652348

American Airlines
C 38 Prem House
Connaught Place
Ph 3316284/3310994

British Airways
DLF Plaza Tower
Qutb Enclave, Gurgaon
Ph 91-6540924
Fax 91-6540547
Airport Ph 5652077/78/
5652908

Cathay Pacific
1st Floor
Kanchenjunga Building
18 Barakhamba Road
Ph 3325789/3321286
Fax 3721550
Airport Ph 5654701-04

Gulf Air
G 12 Marina Arcade
Connaught Circus
Ph 3324293/3327814
Fax 3722944
Airport Ph 5652065

Japan Airlines
36 Chandralok Building
Janpath
Ph 3327104/3327108
Fax 3320586
Airport Ph 5653942/
5653358

KLM
Prakash Deep Building
7 Tolstoy Marg
Ph 3357747 **Fax** 3353279
Airport Ph 5652715/
5654897

Lufthansa
56 Janpath
Ph 3323310/3327268
Fax 3711913
Airport Ph 5652064/
5652328

Royal Nepal Airlines
44 Janpath
Ph 3321164/3323437
Fax 3327127
Airport Ph 5696876

Singapore Airlines
9th Floor Ashoka Estate
Barakhamba Road
Ph 3356286/3326373
Fax 3722115
Airport Ph 5653822/
5653072

Thai Airways
Park Royal Hotel
Nehru Place
Ph 6239988 **Fax** 6239149
Airport Ph 5652413/
5652796

Virgin Atlantic
Room No 5
Janpath Hotel, Janpath
Ph 3343284/85
Airport Ph 5655747-48

Domestic Airlines Offices

Indian Airlines
Malhotra Bldg
F Block, Connaught Place
Ph 3310727

Safdarjang Airport
Aurobindo Marg
Ph 4620566/4620569
(24 hour office)
Airport Ph 5675121

Alliance Air
(a subsidiary of Indian
Airlines)
Airport Ph 5675313

Jet Airways
N 40 Connaught Place
Ph 3321241

13 Community Centre,
Yusuf Sarai **(24 hour office)**
Ph 6853700/6562266
Airport Ph 5675404

Sahara India Airlines
Gopaldas Building
Barakhamba Road
Ph 3326851/3326853

UG 32 Ansal Chambers I
Bhikaji Cama Place
Ph 6188512/6195764
Airport Ph 5675234/
5675357

Airport Enquiry

Domestic Terminal
Ph 5675121/5675126
International Terminal
Ph 5652011/5652021

**The reporting time
for domestic flights
is 60 minutes prior
to departure, and for
international flights
three hours prior
to departure.**

Where to Stay

Delhi has a wide range of accommodation – from deluxe five-star hotels that are as good as the best in the world, through mid-range hotels and guest-houses that are often well-appointed and offer good service and a comfortable stay, to down-market tourist lodges in crowded localities. The budget hotels and budget tourist lodges are mostly located in Connaught Place, Paharganj and in the old city area of Shahjahanabad.

Taxes levied: Do remember that over and above the room rent, there is a hotel entertainment tax on air-conditioned hotels and an additional luxury tax in case of deluxe and five-star hotels. Expenditure tax and a food and beverage tax is also applicable in case of five-star hotels.

Apart from hotels, there are other options that one may consider when selecting a place to stay – guest-houses, railway and airport retiring rooms, *dharamshalas* and *gurudwaras* run by Hindu and Sikh religious trusts. Retiring rooms are available at Delhi Main and New Delhi Railway Stations for upper-class train passengers. There are also dormitory facilities, camping sites and youth hostels for students and travellers

YMCA Tourist Hostel
Jai Singh Road
Connaught Place
Ph 3746031 Fax 3746032

Youth Hostel
5 Nyaya Marg
Chanakyapuri
Ph 6116285
Fax 6113469/4676349

YWCA
Blue Triangle Family Hostel
Ashoka Road
Ph 3360133 Fax 3360202

YWCA International Guest House
10 Sansad Marg
Ph 3361561 Fax 3341763

Basic accommodation is available at the following for a maximum of three days against proof of train journey:

Retiring Rooms
New Delhi Railway Station
Ph 3733222

Rail Yatri Niwas
Ajmeri Gate
Ph 3233484

Given below are names of a few hotels:

Price range in rupees for a standard double room
Ⓐ Above 6000
Ⓑ 4000-6000
Ⓒ 2500-4000
Ⓓ 1500-2500
Ⓔ Below 1500

Ambassador
Sujan Singh Park
Ph 4632600 Fax 4638219 Ⓑ

Ashok (Govt run)
50 B Chanakyapuri
Ph 6110101 Fax 6873216 Ⓐ

Diplomat
9 Sardar Patel Marg
Ph 3010204 Fax 3018605 Ⓑ

Grand Intercontinental
Barakhamba Avenue
Connaught Place
Ph 3411234/3411001
Fax 3412233/3709123 Ⓐ

Grand Hyatt
Nelson Mandela Road
Vasant Kunj Phase-II
Ph 6121234/6771234
Fax 6895891 Ⓐ

Hyatt Regency
Bhikaji Cama Place
Ph 6791234 Fax 6791122 Ⓐ

Imperial
Janpath
Ph 3341234 Fax 3342255 Ⓐ

Indraprastha (Govt run)
19 Ashoka Road
Ph 3344511 Fax 3368153 Ⓔ

Janpath (Govt run)
Janpath
Ph 3340070 Fax 3368618 Ⓓ

Kanishka (Govt run)
Ashoka Road
Ph 3344422
Fax 3368242 Ⓑ

Le Meridien
8 Windsor Place
Ph 3710101 Fax 3714545 Ⓐ

Lodhi (Govt run)
Lala Lajpat Rai Marg
Ph 4361983
Fax 4362082/4360883 Ⓓ

Marina
Connaught Circus
Ph 3324658 Fax 3328609 Ⓒ

Marriott Welcome Hotel
District Centre Saket
Opp. GM Modi Hospital
Saket
Ph 6521122/6521362
Fax 6522112 Ⓐ

Maurya Sheraton
Sardar Patel Marg
Ph 6112233
Fax 6113333 Ⓐ

Metropolitan Nikko
Bangla Sahib Road
Ph 3342000
Fax 3343000 Ⓐ

Nirula's
L Block Connaught Place
Ph 3322419
Fax 3324669 Ⓒ

PRACTICAL INFORMATION

Oberoi
Dr Zakir Hussain Marg
Ph 4363030
Fax 4360484 Ⓐ

Oberoi Maidens
7 Shyam Nath Marg
Ph 3975464
Fax 3890595 Ⓒ

Qutab Hotel (Govt run)
Shaheed Jeet Singh Marg
Ph 6521010
Fax 6960828 Ⓒ

Radisson
National Highway 8
Ph 6779191/6779221
Fax 6779090 Ⓐ

Samrat (Govt run)
Chanakyapuri
Ph 6110606
Fax 6887047 Ⓒ

Siddharth
3 Rajendra Place
Ph 5762501
Fax 5781016 Ⓑ

Taj Palace
Diplomatic Enclave
2 Sardar Patel Marg
Ph 6110202/6110808 Ⓐ

Taj Mahal Hotel
Mansingh Road
Ph 3026162
Fax 3026070 Ⓐ

The Claridges
12 Aurangzeb Road
Ph 3010211
Fax 3010625 Ⓑ

The Connaught
37 Shaheed Bhagat Singh
Marg
Ph 3364225
Fax 3340757 Ⓒ

The Park
Sansad Marg
Ph 3743737
Fax 3744000 Ⓑ

Vikram
Lajpat Nagar
Ph 6436451
Fax 6435657 Ⓓ

Where to Eat

Food from almost all parts of the world is available in Delhi, making it easier for travellers who find it difficult to leave their home cuisine behind. However, the delicacies typical of various parts of India are worth sampling and Delhi offers an amazing variety of food through its many restaurants.

Restaurants within the capital are varied not only in their ambience, or lack of it, but also in their rates.

A sumptuous meal for two could range from less than Rs 200 to an exorbitant sum.

Booking: It is advisable to book a table in a restaurant, especially during the festive season, to avoid a tedious wait or even disappointment. Booking for a table in a restaurant may generally be done from the place of your stay.

Taxes: Certain additional taxes are levied over and above the listed price at air-conditioned restaurants.

Where to Shop

Delhi is a shopper's paradise, a veritable cornucopia of silk, spices, dry fruits and handicrafts. These and much else spill out of its many *bazaars* and markets. There are markets in almost every locality and there is also the occasional specialist shop that deals in a particular variety of exotica.

If you are in Delhi for just a couple of days, it would perhaps be best to head for Connaught Place, the city's best-known market place. It would give you a chance to also take in the state emporia on Baba Kharak Singh Marg, the Central Cottage Industries Emporium on Janpath and the warren of small shops in the underground market at Palika Bazaar.

Major Shopping Complexes

Ambawatta Complex

For those in search of the elegant and the exclusive, the place to go is Ambawatta Complex on the fringe of Mehrauli village. Good Earth Verandah is highly recommended for furniture and furnishings.

Ansal Plaza

Ansal Plaza is a huge shopping complex on Khel Gaon Marg. Inspired by American shopping malls, it is a shopper's paradise. All kinds of Indian and foreign branded goods can be found under one roof. And for the gastronomically inclined there is a wide range of restaurants in the complex.

Central Cottage Industries Emporium

At Central Cottage Industries Emporium in Jawahar

Vyapar Bhawan, Janpath, under one roof you will find a spectacular display of Indian handlooms and handicrafts. Prices are fixed and quality is assured.

Ph 3320439

Dilli Haat

A *haat* is a periodic market and at Dilli Haat crafts-persons come from different parts of the country for a fortnight at a time. It is also the only place in town where regional food from all over India is available.

Ph 6119055/4678817

Palika Bazaar

An underground market in the heart of Connaught Place, this is popular among those on a shoe-string budget.

Santushti Shopping Arcade

Located opposite Samrat Hotel, Santushti has a handful of exclusive shops set in manicured lawns.

Ph 4100108

State Emporia

Eighteen in all, the State Emporia on Baba Kharak Singh Marg showcase handicrafts and handlooms of the states they represent.

Central Market in Lajpat Nagar, Ajmal Khan Road Market in Karol Bagh and Sarojini Nagar Market are very popular with Dilliwalas for inexpensive readymades, attractive cotton yardage and embroidered garments.

South Extension Market, Khan Market and M Block Market in Greater Kailash I are more upmarket and most international brands available in India have their outlets here.

Bookshops

Bahrisons
Khan Market
Ph 4694610

The Bookworm
29 B Connaught Place
Ph 3322260

The Book Shop
Khan Market
Ph 4697102

Childrens' Book Trust
Nehru House
Bahadurshah Zafar Marg
Ph 3316970

E D Galgotia & Sons
B 17 Connaught Place
Ph 3713227

Fact & Fiction
Priya Complex, Vasant Vihar
Ph 6146843

Faqir Chand & Sons
Khan Market **Ph** 4618810

Jain Book Agency
C 9 Connaught Place
Ph 3355686

Midlands
20 Aurobindo Place Market
Ph 6867121

Motilal Banarasi Dass Publishers
40-41 UA Bungalow Road
Jawahar Nagar
Ph 3911985

National Book Trust
A 5 Green Park
Ph 6868562

Rupa & Co
7/16 Ansari Road, Daryaganj
Ph 3270260

Teksons
G 4 South Extension I
Ph 4617030

Variety Book Depot
M 3 AVG Bhawan
Middle Circle
Connaught Place
Ph 3327175/3344567

Market Holidays

Sunday	Azad Market, Baba Kharak Singh Marg, Chandni Chowk, Chawri Bazaar, Connaught Place, Hauz Khas Village, Janpath, Khan Market, Khari Baoli, Meena Bazaar, Nai Sarak, Nehru Place, Paharganj, Palika Bazaar, Sadar Bazaar, Sabzi Mandi, Shanker Market, Yashwant Place.
Monday	Ajmal Khan Road, Defence Colony Market, INA Market, Karol Bagh, Lajpat Nagar Central Market, Nizamuddin, Sarojini Nagar Market, South Extension.
Tuesday	Aurobindo Place, C R Park, Greater Kailash, Green Park, Hauz Khas, Munirka, New Friends Colony, R K Puram, Vasant Vihar, Masoodpur, Vasant Kunj, Yusuf Sarai.
Wednesday	Tilak Nagar, Rajouri Garden

Shopping Hours: 10 am to 7 pm

FURTHER READING

Brown, Percy, *Indian Architecture (Islamic Period)*, Mumbai, 1997.

Chandra, Satish, *Medieval India*, Delhi, 1990.

Eraly, Abraham, *Emperors of the Peacock Throne: The Saga of the Great Mughals*, Delhi, 2000.

Fanshawe, H C, *Shah Jahan's Delhi: Past and Present*, London, 1902.

Gascoigne, Bamber, *The Great Moghuls*, Delhi, 1987.

Gupta, Narayani, *Our City: Delhi*, Delhi, 1987.

Kaul, H K, *Historic Delhi: An Anthology*, Delhi, 1985.

Kaye, M M, *The Golden Calm: An English Lady's Life in Moghul Delhi*, New York, 1980.

Koch, Ebba, *Mughal Architecture*, Delhi, 2002.

Lowry, G D, 'Humayun's Tomb: Form Function and Meaning in Early Mughal Architecture', in Grabar Oleg (ed.), *Muqarnas*, Vol. IV, Leiden, 1987.

Mitra, Swati (ed.), *Delhi: City Guide*, Delhi, 2002.

Mitra, Swati (ed.), *Speaking Stones: World Cultural Heritage Sites in India*, Delhi, 2000.

Naqvi, S A A, *Humayun's Tomb and Adjacent Buildings*, Delhi, 1947.

Nath, R, *History of Mughal Architecture*, Vol I, Delhi, 1982.

Sharma, P K, *Mughal Architecture of Delhi*, Delhi, 2000.

Sharma, Y D, *Delhi and its Neighbourhood*, Delhi, 1990 (Reprint).

Spear, Percival, *Delhi, its Monuments and History*, updated and annotated by Narayani Gupta and Laura Sykes, Delhi, 1994.

Stephen, Carr, *The Archaeology and Monumental Remains of Delhi*, Delhi, 2002.

Tillotson, G H R, *Mughal India*, London, 1991.

Zafar Hasan, *List of Hindu and Muhammadan Monuments*, Vol II, Calcutta, 1919.

GLOSSARY

bagh garden

baoli stepped well

bracket projecting ornament or support

bulbous shaped like a bulb, nearly spherical

burj tower

chabutra raised platform

chamferred where a right-angled corner is given a flat face

charbagh four-fold garden

chhajja overhanging eave

chhattri umbrella-like kiosks acting as turrets on roofs

clerestory a raised section of the roof with windows in it

corbelled blocks of stones projecting from a wall

cupola spherical roof

cusped projecting point between the small arcs of an archway

dalan rear chamber

double dome composed of two shells, an inner and an outer

drum circular wall on which a dome rests

finial finishing portion of a pinnacle

gumbad dome

iwan arched recess

jali literally net; lattice or perforated pattern

jharokha window embrasures

keystone central stone of a true arch

merlons solid part of a battlement

mihrab a niche or arched recess in the western wall of an Indian mosque, towards which the worshippers turn for prayers

parterres level space in a garden occupied by flower beds

sarai rest house

spandrels the triangular space between the curve of an arch and the square enclosing it

squinch a device of arches placed diagonally at the upper angles of a square chamber with the aim of turning it into an octagon and then capping it with a dome

supurdgah temporary tomb

trabeate construction using beams and lintels to bridge space

vault arched covering over any space

INDEX

Below:
South face of Humayun's Tomb